MACDONALD STARTERS

D1346569

The Sea

Macdonald Educational

About Macdonald Starters

Macdonald Starters are vocabulary controlled information books for young children. More than ninety per cent of the words in the text will be in the reading vocabulary of the vast majority of young readers. Word and sentence length have also been carefully controlled.

Key new words associated with the topic of each book are repeated with picture explanations in the Starters dictionary at the end. The dictionary can also be used as an index for teaching children to look things up.

Teachers and experts have been consulted on the content and accuracy of the books.

Illustrated by: Bermejo

Editors: Peter Usborne, Su Swallow Jennifer Vaughan

Reading consultant: Donald Moyle, author of *The Teaching of Reading* and senior lecturer in education at Edge Hill College of Education

Chairman, teacher advisory panel: F. F. Blackwell, general inspector for schools, London Borough of Croydon, with responsibility for primary education

Teacher panel: Elizabeth Wray, Loveday Harmer, Lynda Snowdon, Joy West

First published 1971 by Macdonald and Company (Publishers) Limited
St Giles House
49-50 Poland Street
London W1

I am sitting on a rock.
The rock is on the seashore.
The waves splash the rock.

1

My Daddy is going to swim
under the sea.
He puts on his goggles.

Now Daddy is swimming.
He floats on the sea.
He can see under the water.

He can see little fish.
The fish swim into the seaweed.
The seaweed grows
on the bottom of the sea.
4

Now Daddy has swum further out.
The water is deeper.
Bigger fish live here.

The sea is shallow
near the land.
The sea is very deep
far from land.

There are mountains in the sea.
Sometimes the tops of mountains
make islands.

Many fish and plants
live near the surface.
There is light near the surface.
Plants need light to live.

There is no light
where the sea is very deep.
No plants live there.
Only some strange fish live there.

This is a diver.
He breathes air from a tube.
His suit keeps him dry.

These machines go down very deep.
They go deeper than divers.
Men sit inside.
They explore the deep sea.

This is a little submarine.
A man holds on to it.
He explores the shallow water.

This is an atomic submarine.
The captain uses the periscope
to see above the water.

In some places there is ice
all over the sea.
Atomic submarines
can go under the ice.
14

Huge bits of ice break off.
These are called icebergs.
This ship hit an iceberg and sank.

15

Ships can sink in storms too.
In storms the wind blows the sea
into big waves.

16

Waves break on the shore.
Big waves make a loud noise.
They make spray too.

When it is high tide
the sea comes up the beach.
When it is low tide
it goes down again.

18

This castle is on an island.
When the tide goes down
people can walk to it.

All sea water is salty.
Things float well in salty water.
The Dead Sea is very salty.
You can nearly sit up in it.

In some places
the sun dries the sea water up.
The salt is left.
Men collect the salt.

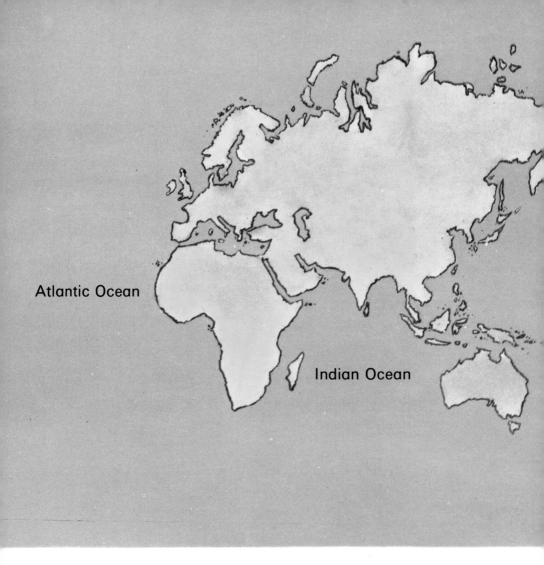

Atlantic Ocean

Indian Ocean

Here is a map of the world.
Here are the names
of the big oceans.
22

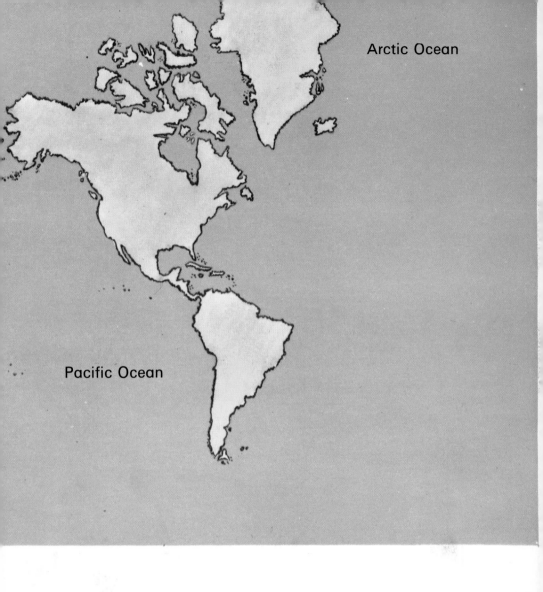

Arctic Ocean

Pacific Ocean

See if you can read them.

Starter's **The Sea** words

rock
(page 1)

goggles
(page 2)

waves
(page 1)

seaweed
(page 4)

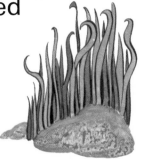

swim
(page 2)

island
(page 7)

diver
(page 10)

atomic submarine
(page 14)

submarine
(page 12)

iceberg
(page 15)

captain
(page 13)

periscope
(page 13)

sink
(page 15)

shore
(page 17)

castle
(page 19)

spray
(page 17)

float
(page 20)

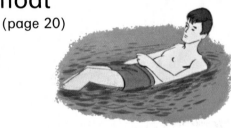

high tide
(page 18)

salt
(page 21)

low tide
(page 18)

map
(page 22)

26